984

S0-ATZ-256

Happy 31st
Birthday with Love
love
04

F ROM
THE BEGINNING
of civilization, human imagination
gave birth to creatures never actually
seen upon the earth or in the air.
Of all these mythical beings,
one of them is so richly symbolic
that for the last five thousand years,
artists have shaped and reshaped it
in materials from stone to lace.
This majestic beast
has pulled the chariots of gods,
guarded ancient treasures, cured human illness
with its magic claws, pursued sinners.
It has been the subject of
travelers' tales and scientists' doubts
and regarded as an animal of whimsy.
Part lion, part eagle...

The Book of
GRYPHONS

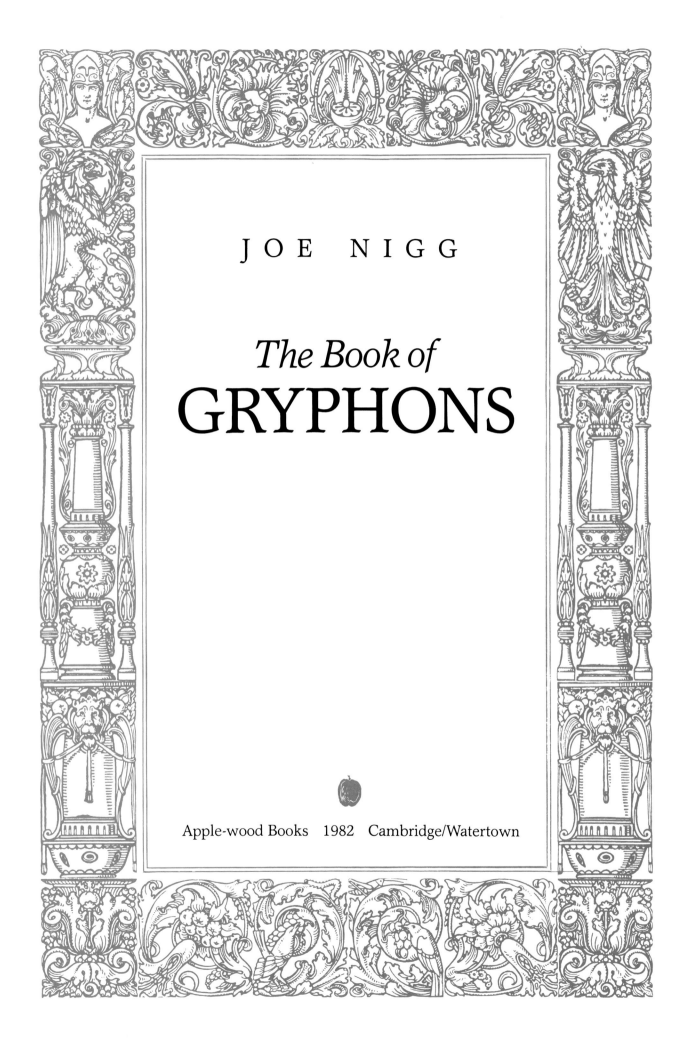

JOE NIGG

The Book of
GRYPHONS

Apple-wood Books   1982   Cambridge/Watertown

The Book of Gryphons
Copyright © 1982 by Joe Nigg

ISBN:0-918222-37-0 Cloth

Design: Martha Lehtola-Swanson
Photo Research: Gail F. Page
Composition: The Beckler Press, Boston, Massachusetts
Printing: Merchants Press, Boston, Massachusetts

In addition to the above, the author would like to offer
special thanks to Esther Muzzillo for her generous help
through all stages of the research and writing of the text,
and he extends his appreciation to all who took an interest
in this book, especially Zohn Artman, Dr. Haroula
Tzavella-Evjen, James Nelson, and Miles Thompson.

All rights reserved.
Printed in the United States of America.
No part of this book may be used or reproduced in any
manner whatsoever without written permission, except in the
case of brief quotations embodied in critical articles and
reviews. For information write to Apple-wood Books, Inc.,
Box 2870, Cambridge, Massachusetts 02139.

1 2 3 4 5 6 7 8 9 10

For Joey and Mike

Contents

CHAPTER ONE

Master of Two Worlds

WHEN WE CONSIDER that most people still believed in imaginary animals three hundred years ago, it is easy for us to feel quite enlightened. At the same time, we seriously talk about the existence of Bigfoot, the Abominable Snowman, and the Loch Ness Monster, and concoct shapes of life beyond our planet.

Without knowing the forms of actual creatures, we would be no more surprised to see a Gryphon than a lion or an eagle; no more surprised to see a unicorn than an ibex, a dragon than an iguana. And we would be no more surprised to see

Opposite: Ashur, the Assyrian god of war and empire.

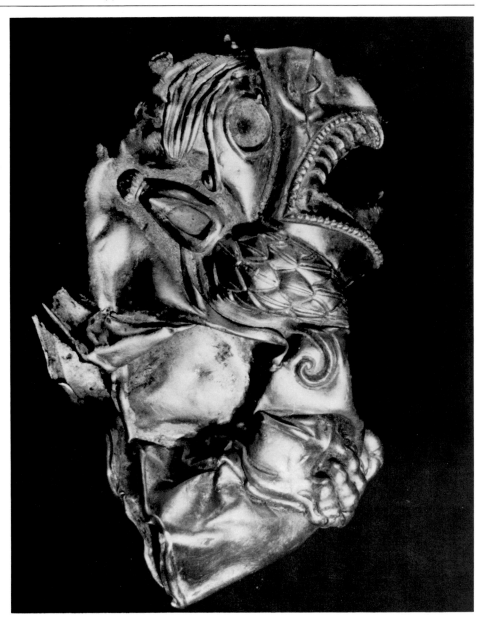

Above: The Gryphon was the guardian of ancient treasures. This golden Gryphon head was part of an Assyrian treasure now known as the Ziwiyeh Horde. Buried about 600 B.C., in 1946 these treasures were discovered accidentally by a shepherd boy in northwestern Iran.

nearly any mythical beast than to see a spotted creature on stilt-like legs whose neck is so long the animal can eat leaves off of treetops; or a leathery, rotund beast whose elongated, rubbery nose seems to have been stretched out of its head; or the kangaroo, the armadillo, the praying mantis, and on through the animal kingdom. Given the infinite variety of the animal world, people of the past naturally accepted the existence of animals we are now certain are fabulous.

How Imaginary Beasts Are Born

There are many theories about the origin of imaginary beasts. The creation of fantastic creatures has been regarded as a

way people of early civilizations made what was unknown and unseen more controllable and less frightening.

One literal explanation for the existence of fabulous creatures is that man's discovery of bones of animals un-familiar to him—perhaps the bones of prehistoric animals such as the dinosaur and the pterodactyl—caused him to conjure up images of creatures that never were. The tusks of an ex-tinct Siberian beast, for example, were regarded as Gryphon claws.

A charming ancient theory about the origin of fabulous be-ings can be found in the work of the Roman poet and philosopher, Lucretius. Lucretius believed that all matter is

Above: Also made of gold, the Gryphon head on the left is a detail from the Greek earring on the right. This ornament, from the Archaic period, was worn by suspending it from a thin wire passed through the ear lobe.

Above: Greek tomb painting of Gryphons from Paestum in southern Italy, fourth century B.C.

composed of atoms, as we believe today, but some of his other theories we would now consider whimsical. One of his notions was that images which enter the mind come from flimsy films of atoms which fly off the surface of things in all directions. When they meet in the mind, he said, they form images of creatures that never before existed, as when a flimsy film of the image of a horse combines with the image-film of a man, creating a centaur, or when three heads unite with

the body of a single dog, making Cerberus, the three-headed guardian of the underworld.

There may, in fact, be something of a mechanical composite process in the formation of fabulous beasts. Such creatures are often composed of the most impressive parts of various animals—parts such as beaks, horns, claws, wings, and tails. The imagination constructs these animals into new beings with recognizable parts of real animals. But in the most elemental

figures, such as the Gryphon, the qualities and powers of those creatures are symbolically fused into a single being.

Lewis Thomas, a twentieth-century microbiologist, has compared bacteria, protozoa, and other microorganisms to the creatures of the mythical imagination, maintaining that the process of fusion is a natural one. He believes that living things tend to combine with each other and that any living cell, under the right conditions, can fuse with any other, like the mythical beings of old.

And so, from colliding films of atoms or fusing cells, the Gryphon is born—a combination of lion, king of beasts, and eagle, monarch of the air.

What Is a Gryphon?

Because it has lived so long and in so many places, the Gryphon has appeared with many variations, its personality and shape changing from culture to culture, reflecting the values and beliefs of a given society. What is in its eyes is a short history of the world.

It has had a panther's, dog's, and lion's hind-quarters and a serpent's tail. It has been with and without wings. Golden ray-like spikes have spread from its joints, and its shoulders have been covered with a lion's mane. It has had both lion's and eagle's forefeet and has had the head of a hawk and the

Above: At left, a Gryphon image embroidered on a Coptic textile fragment. On the right, a fragment of a silk shroud from eleventh-century Persia.

Opposite: Two examples of illustrations from Swiss block-printed books of the late-fifteenth century.

Above: A twelfth-century Gryphon-headed pitcher from Lorraine.

Preceding page: A detail from a wool tapestry made in Basel in about 1470. On the left of the wall hanging is the coat of arms of Beatrix Von Hunwil; on the right is the coat of arms of Michael Von Ampringen.

head of an eagle. It has often had a tuft under its beak. It has had a soft, curved beak and a sharp, hooked one, both closed and open, and, inside of the beak, a tongue or teeth. Its eyes have been the eyes of a bird of prey and of the peacock, its ears sharp and pointed like a horse's ears, or floppy like a spaniel's. It has worn a peacock crest, ram's horns, crowns, a decorative knob; and ringlets have hung down its neck. All these variations have given the Gryphon a number of different traits: watchful, loyal, rapacious, strong, swift, graceful, vengeful, and even gentle.

Given the Gryphon's variety, it is hardly surprising that writers have described the beast in many ways. The

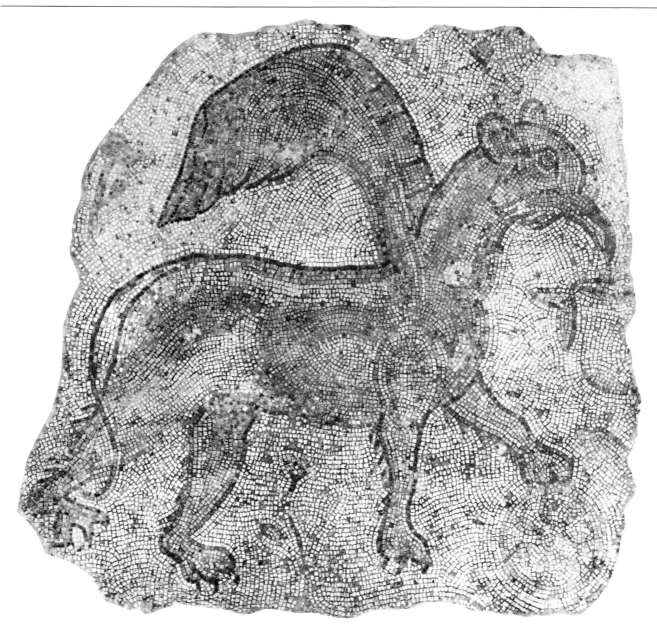

seventeenth-century poet, Robert Chester, depicted the Gryphon as "a bird rich feathered" whose "head is like a lion," while Dr. Samuel Johnson wrote in his *Dictionary* that the Gryphon is "a fabled animal, said to be generated between the lion and the eagle and to have the head and paws of the lion and the wings of an eagle." According to these descriptions, the Gryphon is a lion-headed bird or a winged lion.

One scholar classifies the beast into the families of the bird-griffin, the snake-griffin, and the lion-griffin. Another scholar explains that lions with wings and at least two birds' feet are called lion-griffins. But these he prefers to call dragons, along with snake-griffins, which have the tails of serpents.

Above: Byzantine mosaic of a Gryphon from fifth-century Syria. This piece is shown in color on the dedication page.

This confusing variety of Gryphon shapes is paralleled by the number of spellings of the beast's name: *griffin, griffon, gryphon, griffun, gryfoun(e), griffown, griffoun(e), greffon, gryffon, grifon, gryfon, griffion, griffen, gryffen, griffyn, grefyne, grifyn, gryffin, griphon, girphinne, grephoun, griphin, grephoun, griphin, gryphin,* and *gryphen.* The word comes from the French *griffon,* the Old French *grifoun,* the Italian *grifone,* the Latin *gryphus,* the Greek *grups,* and possibly from the Hebrew word for "cherub."

Because of all these variations, the Gryphon is more difficult to identify than one would think. But there are certain characteristics that make the Gryphon easily recognizable.

In *Alice's Adventures in Wonderland*, when the Queen and Alice come upon the Gryphon lying asleep in the sun, Lewis Carroll, in his own voice, says to the reader: "If you don't know what a Gryphon is, look at the picture." What the reader of the original edition sees is John Tenniel's illustration of the basic Gryphon: a fabulous creature with a long lion tail, lion hind-quarters, eagle wings and forefeet and head, pointed ears, and a tuft of beard under its beak.

Above: John Tenniel's illustration of the basic Gryphon. From Lewis Carroll's Alice's Adventures in Wonderland.

Opposite: At the top is a Luristan cheek piece, one of a pair, from seventh or eighth century B.C., used on a horse's bit. Below, a simurgh depicted on a plate.

The Gryphon Family

GIANT BIRDS   Throughout the world are legends of fabulous gigantic birds, *Wundervogel*, which were inspired, some say,

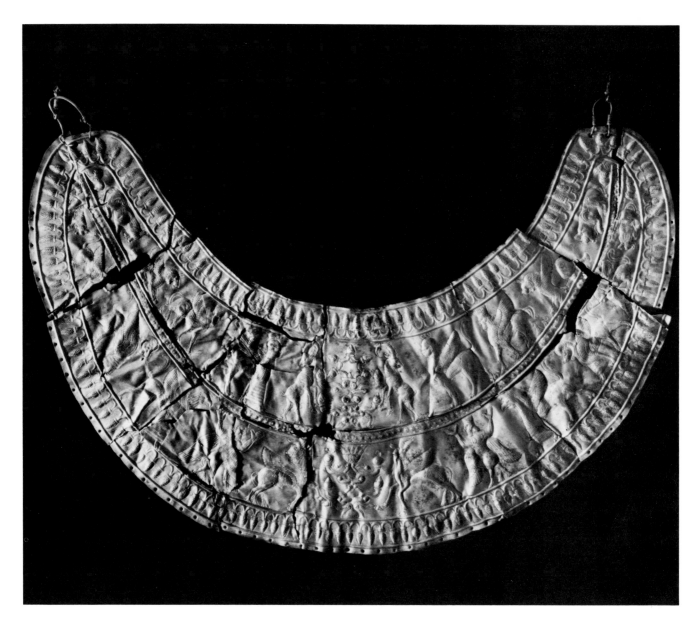

Above: A chest ornament from the Ziwiyeh Horde showing many different fantastic creatures.

Opposite: Above is a detail from the chest ornament shown on the left hand page. At the bottom is a copper gilt plaque from thirteenth-century France showing a Gryphon among other beasts.

by the bones of the prehistoric pterodactyl or by actual birds such as the condor. Most of these mythical birds are so large and strong that they can carry people, oxen, elephants, and horses and riders. Some of them guard fabulous treasure. Some are intermediaries between earth and heaven. Some devour humans, while others are benefactors of mankind.

The Senmurv, an ancient Persian dog-bird, is an intermediary between heaven and earth and may have symbolized the union of the two. Its home is a tree guarded by spirits, and every time the senmurv lands on the tree's branches, thousands of seeds are scattered over the earth and cure the illnesses of mankind.

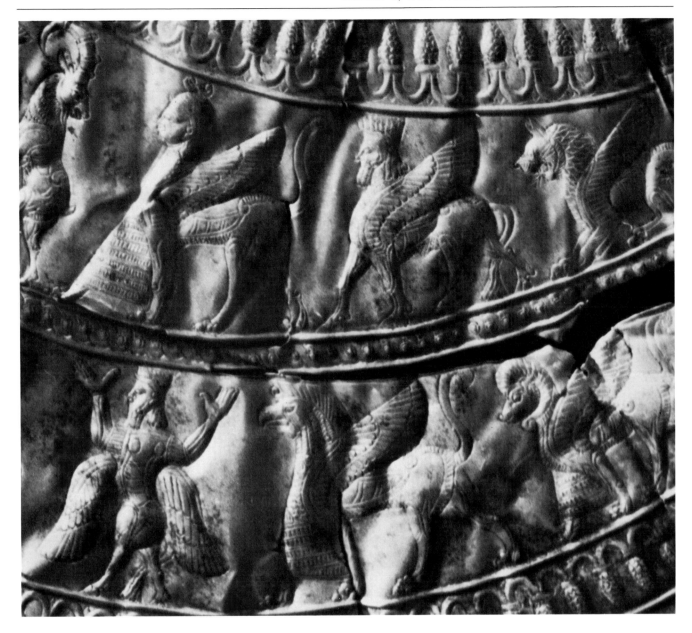

The Simurgh, perhaps a transformation of the senmurv, appeared in an eleventh-century Persian epic poem, *The Shah Nameh*, by Firdausi. To Sam, a warrior, a son is born, whose hair is white. Believing his son, Zal, is a progeny of demons, Sam takes the boy to the mountain Alberz and abandons him. Alberz is the home of the simurgh, the all-knowing Bird of Ages, who is rational and has the power of speech. The simurgh finds the child and carries him to its mountain nest, where it raises and teaches the boy. Years later, Sam dreams that Zal is still alive and, guilt-ridden over abandoning his son, prays for forgiveness and for Zal's return. Hearing the lament of the father, the simurgh explains to Zal that he must return

Above: Edward W. Lane's illustration of a roc from The Arabian Nights' Entertainments.

to his father and, as proof of its affection, gives Zal a feather from its own wing, explaining that whenever Zal is in trouble, he should throw the feather into a fire and the simurgh will appear. Zal returns to his father's kingdom, rules wisely, and marries. When his wife is about to bear a child, she becomes deathly ill. Remembering the simurgh's feather, Zal throws it into the fire. The simurgh appears, cures the woman, and she bears the great hero Rustam, the Persian Hercules.

The Roc (Rukh), like the simurgh, is gigantic, but unlike the wise and kind old Bird of Ages, it is rapacious and much feared. The two birds together exemplify the dual nature of the Gryphon, which is both gracious and malevolent.

On his second voyage, in *The Arabian Nights*, Sindbad is alone on an island near a great white dome which he discovers is an egg of the gigantic Roc, a monster which feeds its young on elephants. To escape from the island, Sindbad ties his turban around his waist and to one of the talons of the nesting Roc. The Roc awakes and takes to flight, carrying Sindbad through the void, soaring higher and higher until it almost touches the heavens. When the bird alights on a hillside overlooking a valley, Sindbad escapes, and the Roc, picking up a great serpent in its beak, flies away. Sindbad descends to the valley, which is blazing with light, and there finds the ground covered with diamonds. But coiling among the gems

Above: This illustration by Edmund Dulac of the second voyage of Sinbad the Sailor shows Sinbad suspended from the gigantic roc's talon.

Above: From The Arabian Nights' Entertainments, *a nineteenth-century woodcut of a roc, after an original design by William Harvey.*

are deadly vipers, which are able to swallow whole elephants in a single gulp.

In Marco Polo's *Travels*, a popular book of the Middle Ages which purported to be a traveler's true account of exotic lands, Marco Polo hears about some southerly islands seldom visited because "gryphon birds," which the natives call "rukhs," appear there in certain seasons.

Another early traveler, Ibn Batuta, wrote in his journal one day in the China Seas that, "What we took for a mountain is the rukh! If it sees us it will send us to destruction." But he added later that God "sent us a fair wind which turned us from the direction in which the rukh was." And in 1579,

Thomas Twyne wrote, "About the Indian sea there is a certain bird of incredible bigness, whom our countrymen call a Roche, which is able and accustomed to take up, not only a man, but also a whole ship in her beak."

OTHER RELATIVES OF THE GRYPHON The Opinicus, in heraldry, is sometimes regarded as a debased Gryphon. It has the forelegs of a lion rather than the forelegs of an eagle. Also, its tail is thin and short, with a small tuft at the end, more like a camel's than a lion's. The opinicus is on the crest of the coat of arms belonging to the Company of the Barber Surgeons of the City of London and is also on the arms granted, in the

Above: An opinicus graces a section of a Roman architectural panel.

Above and opposite: Two of Gustave Dore's illustrations of the Hippogryph in Orlando Furioso.

twentieth century, to Sir Frederick Treve, the surgeon who performed a successful appendectomy on King Edward VII.

The Hippogryph is the offspring of the Gryphon and the horse. The hippogryph is the creation of a single known writer, Ariosto, an Italian Renaissance poet, who devised the beast for his epic, *Orlando Furioso*. In classical tradition, the Gryphon is the mortal enemy of the horse. Ariosto mated the improbable pair, inspired by a line from Virgil's *Eclogues*: "Now griffins will be mated with horses." In *Orlando Furioso* Ariosto joins the two as a symbol of love. The offspring, the hippogryph, belongs to the magician Atlantes, who teaches the hero Rogero to ride the beast with a magic bridle.

Above: At left, a Greek drinking cup from 540 B.C. showing sphinxes and a Gryphon-bird on the right. The cup was painted by a Greek artist known as the "Gryphon-Bird Painter." On the right is a Greek bowl, from approximately 560 B.C., showing a sphinx and two panthers.

As a variation of the flying horse, the hippogryph is related to the Greek Pegasus, to Odin's eight-legged steed, Sleipner, and to the silver horse Mohammed rode from Mecca.

The Sphinx was born about the same time as the Gryphon. Like the Gryphon, this ancient figure has varied from culture to culture. The sphinx probably originated in Egypt, where it was portrayed as a recumbent lion with a human or animal head. The falcon-headed sphinx differs from the Gryphon only in the absence of wings. The Egyptian sphinx represented the sun god and the power of the Pharoah and was often the guardian of temples. The Great Sphinx of Giza, 189 feet long, guards the entrance to the Nile valley.

Above: A chimera from the seventh or eighth century B.C., used on a cheek piece of a horse's bit.

In its association with the sun and kingship, and in its role as guardian, the sphinx is similar to the Gryphon. With and without wings, it was popular in ancient art throughout the Near East and is even found in the Mayan culture in Yucatan. In story, it is famous for its riddle: "What is four-footed, two-footed, and three-footed?" The beast is man himself, passing through infancy, adulthood and cane-aided old age. Because of the many similarities between the sphinx and the Gryphon, some writers have speculated that these two mythical beings originated from the same source.

The Dragon is another ancient beast of the imagination. Like the Gryphon, it is, at times, a fierce, winged guardian of

Above: The Chinese Gryphon-headed jug on the left is from the T'ang dynasty. On the right, the porcelain vase from seventeenth-century China shows a dragon which closely resembles a Gryphon.

Opposite: A woodcut by Peter Wagener done in the fifteenth or sixteenth century shows a male Gryphon during an eclipse of the sun.

treasure, leading some writers to suggest that these two beasts have a common origin. The dragon has appeared around the world through the ages, but unlike the Gryphon and the sphinx, it has not retained an essential form. It has been portrayed with various numbers of legs and heads and has been composed of the parts of many different animals. Overall, though, we tend to think of the dragon as being reptilian and with spiny, rather than feathered, wings.

CHAPTER TWO

Sacred to the Sun

A LONG WITH A HOST of other fabulous creatures, the Gryphon was born in the human imagination around 3,000 B.C. in the ancient Near East. Because visual images of things come before words, the Gryphon was portrayed in pictures before it appeared in stories.

Currently regarded as the earliest known Gryphon, dating back to the third millennium, is a seal-impression from Susa, the capital of ancient Elam, in what is now Iran. The seal-impression has the basic Gryphon form: lion hindparts, wings, and the head and forefeet of a bird of prey.

Opposite: The Gryphon of Nemesis, god of justice in Greek mythology.

Egyptian Gryphons

Above: Belt buckles. On the Frankish buckle in the center of the page, a Gryphon drinks from a fountain.

Below: An impression of a gem shows Helios and his Gryphon-drawn chariot.

In Egypt, the Gryphon's form evolved slowly. On a cosmetic palette from the third millennium B.C. is an early image of the Gryphon: gangly, uncertain. In the Twelfth Dynasty (2000-1788 B.C.) tomb-paintings of Beni-Hasan, male and female Gryphons are majestic guards. Each has the head of the Sacred Hawk, the embodiment of the sun.

By the Seventeenth Dynasty (1600-1580 B.C.), the fabulous beast wore the White Crown, or *Atef*, of the god Osiris. As Pharoah's champion, the Gryphon conquered the enemies of the kingdom.

All through Egyptian art the Gryphon was associated with the sun, with kingship, and with death. It was guardian and protector: loyal, vigilant, and vengeful.

Above: Intaglio impressions of Gryphons from Babylonia, Assyria, and Greece. As the protector of the riches of nations, the Gryphon was often emblazoned on the faces of coins, as in the two examples of coins on the left.

Minoan Gryphons

Sir Arthur Evans, a British archeologist who uncovered the Minoan civilization, believed that the Gryphon in early Egyptian art strongly influenced the Minoan Gryphon and that later Egyptian art—which portrays the Gryphon with the head of an eagle rather than the head of a hawk—was, in turn, influenced by the Minoan Gryphon. Throughout the first quarter of the twentieth century, Sir Arthur spent a fortune excavating

Above: A Minoan sarcophagus with a gabled lid. The Gryphon is often depicted on coffins to protect the dominion of the dead.

and restoring Minoan Crete. In the Palace of Minos, at Knossos, he discovered some of the most remarkable Gryphons of antiquity.

According to the ancient myth, King Minos's wife, Pasiphae, bears a man-bull monster sired by a white bull from the sea. Shamed by the birth of this monstrous Minotaur, Minos has his artist Daedalus construct a labyrinth in which to hide the beast.

Sir Arthur believed that the Palace of Minos, with its complex passageways, was itself the source of the legend of the labyrinth. What Sir Arthur found there were fresco friezes decorating two pairs of wall-sections, presenting "two couchant

Above: A Rhodian vase with Gryphons.

Griffins, guarding in one case a vision of the Goddess herself and her divine associates on the altar ledge beyond, in the other the seat of honour of her terrestrial vicegerent, the Priest-king."

The graceful bodies of these guardians, lying between papyrus shoots, are pale yellow with tails of a faint blue. Their shoulders are black, red, and blue, with spirals leading into rosettes where wings would begin. Evans points out the unique absence of wings, suggesting that may be due to some assimilation with the Egyptian sphinx. He also contends that the cross-hatched shading of their bodies is the first use of chiaroscuro in the history of art. Their crests are colored

Above: On the right is a detail from the third- or fourth-century Iranian plate shown on the left.

peacock plumes; their blue eyes are akin to the eyes of a peacock. From the colored fragments and patterns of the paintings, the entire frieze was restored.

The Minoan Gryphon is portrayed as having a special sacred association with the Minoan goddess, Evans thought. In addition to guarding the throne, Gryphons are on the doorway leading to an inner shrine, and there is another frieze in which Gryphons are tethered to a column representing the Goddess. There is also a Minoan motif of priests leading Gryphons, and in a scene of the dead entering the Elysian Fields, female figures with Gryphon heads lead the departed to an enthroned Gryphon with the Goddess standing behind it.

In a painting on a sarcophagus from a tomb in the Cretan palace of Hagia Triada, two Gryphons pull two women in a chariot. The women are thought to be goddesses, and the scene has been interpreted as a symbolic representation of the heavenly journey.

Above: Two pair of bronze cheek pieces of horses' bits from seventh-century B.C. Luristan.

Other Gryphons of the Ancient World

At Tell Halaf, in Mesopotamia, the Gryphon is associated with another diety, the Great Goddess of Tell Halaf, a goddess of the night, who ruled the darkness of the heavens and the underworld. The Tell Halaf Gryphon was sculpted from black basalt and has white limestone eyes with black pupils. It has

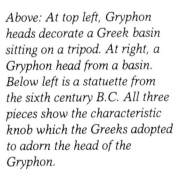

Above: At top left, Gryphon heads decorate a Greek basin sitting on a tripod. At right, a Gryphon head from a basin. Below left is a statuette from the sixth century B.C. All three pieces show the characteristic knob which the Greeks adopted to adorn the head of the Gryphon.

been interpreted as both a bird of the sun and a symbol of the night sky.

The Gryphon appeared on Babylonian cylinder seals, on Assyrian walls, on the monumental capitals of columns at Persepolis, on the border of the oldest rug in the world. It appeared on ivories, on vases, on breastplates and helmets, and as gold clothing ornaments. At Ziwiyeh, a conical knob grew from its head, anticipating the Greek treatment of the beast.

In Greece, and also in Rome, the Gryphon continued to be associated with dieties—and with chariots. Because the Gryphon was associated with the sun, it is hardly surprising

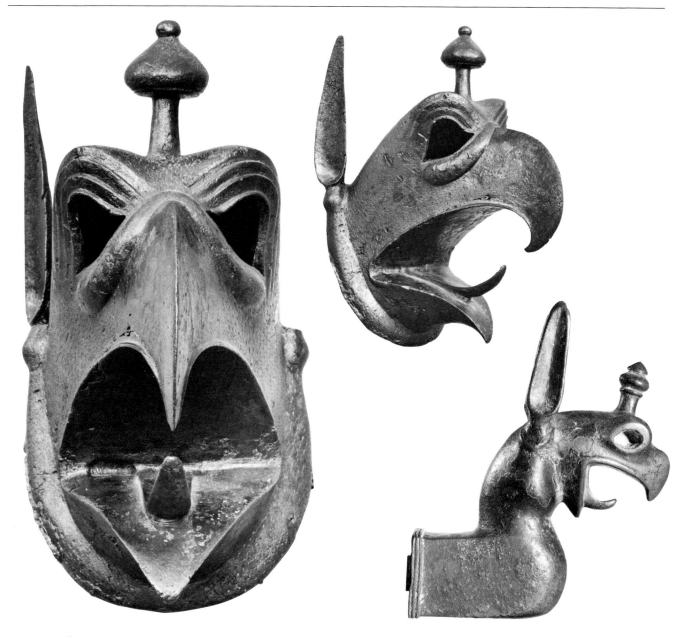

that it became linked with Apollo, pulling that bright god's chariot of the sun. On an Orphic sacramental bowl from Rumania in the third or fourth century A.D., a Gryphon sits at the feet of Hyperborean Apollo, the Lord of Day and Night, who is seated on a throne, holding a lyre, next to his companion.

Consistent with the Gryphon's double nature, the beast also pulls the chariot of the Greek god Nemesis, the avenger of human crimes, who in Roman art is a winged goddess with a whip or sword in her hand, driving her Gryphon-drawn chariot. In sculpture and on Greek coins, the Gryphon is often seen beside a chariot wheel.

Above: At the left and top right, two views of a Gryphon head. At bottom right, this Gryphon head was used to decorate the end of a chariot's pole.

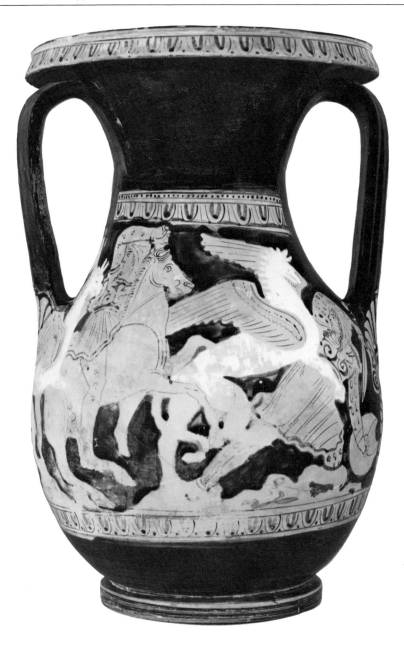

The Arimaspians

Above: A Greek red-figured, covered vase from mid-fourth century B.C. is illustrated with the story of the Arimaspians.

A well-known ancient story portrays the Gryphon as a guardian of Scythian (or Indian) treasure, in continual warfare with the fierce, one-eyed Arimaspians, who attempt to steal the gold. At the Theater of Dionysus, in Athens, this conventionalized scene appears in low relief on the base of the central throne.

References to the fable are common in the work of ancient writers. Herodotus, the "Father of History," credits the story to the Issedonians, who "told of the one-eyed race of men and the gold-guarding griffins."

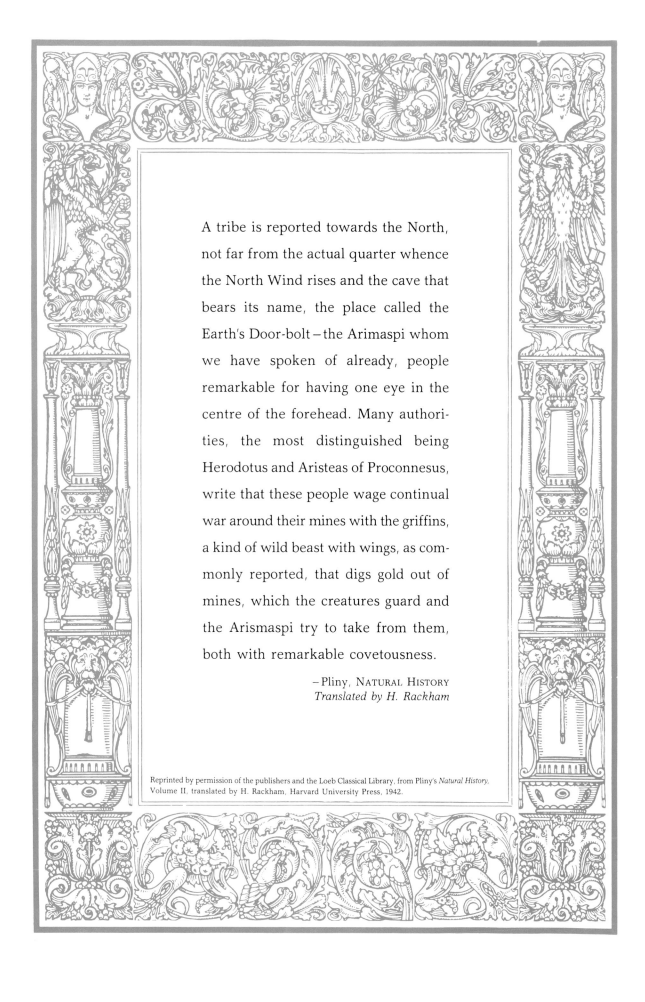

A tribe is reported towards the North, not far from the actual quarter whence the North Wind rises and the cave that bears its name, the place called the Earth's Door-bolt — the Arimaspi whom we have spoken of already, people remarkable for having one eye in the centre of the forehead. Many authorities, the most distinguished being Herodotus and Aristeas of Proconnesus, write that these people wage continual war around their mines with the griffins, a kind of wild beast with wings, as commonly reported, that digs gold out of mines, which the creatures guard and the Arismaspi try to take from them, both with remarkable covetousness.

— Pliny, NATURAL HISTORY
Translated by H. Rackham

Reprinted by permission of the publishers and the Loeb Classical Library, from Pliny's *Natural History*, Volume II, translated by H. Rackham, Harvard University Press, 1942.

Above: The Throne Room at the Palace of Minos at Knossos, showing part of the Gryphon fresco.

Several other classical writers, though, simply repeat the Gryphon story as though it were true. Pomponius Mela writes that, beyond Riphey, where the snow falls continually, "is a country of a very rich soil, but uninhabitable notwithstanding because the Griffons (a cruel and eager kind of wild beast) do wonderfully love the gold, which lies discovered above the ground, and do wonderfully keep it, and are very fierce upon them that touch it." And Solinus calls the Scythian Gryphons "a most fierce kind of fowl, and cruel beyond all cruelty," creatures that "punish the rashness of covetous folk."

Virtually everyone who writes about the Gryphon mentions its warfare with the Arimaspians, for it is a highlight of the

Gryphon's history, dramatizing the beast's vigilance and feroc-ity. As the story is repeated, it becomes more elaborate in detail. Combining the work of many writers, we find that Scythia was the richest ancient source of gold and that Gryphons, whose instinct led them to treasure, roamed the Caucasus Mountains in search of gold and precious stones. The Gryphons would dig up these riches with their power-ful claws, roll about in them with delight, and then sit and watch their treasure for hours, fascinated by the gold and gems shining in sunlight and moonlight. They built their nests of gold and laid in them not eggs, but agates. In that same country lived the one-eyed Arimaspians, who tried to steal

Above: A detail from a painting on a sarcophagus, showing a Gryphon pulling a chariot. This is an early depiction of a scene which recurs many times in classical and medieval art.

Above: A pair of Gryphons attack their traditional enemy. This scene is carved into the side of a fourth-century B.C. Etruscan sarcophagus.

Opposite: At top, a full view of the scene that is portrayed on the side of the fourteenth-century B.C. Greek ivory cosmetic box below.

the Gryphon gold for the adornment of their hair. They attacked the Gryphons on horses, which led to the hostility between the Gryphon and the horse, but the ferocious Gryphons, so strong they could carry off a horse and rider together, either tore the Arimaspians to pieces or carried them back to the Gryphon nests and fed them to their young.

By this time in history, the major aspects of the Gryphon's dual nature had been established. On the one hand, the Gryphon was the guardian and consort of kings and gods—guarding tombs and thrones, pulling chariots; on the other hand, the Gryphon crushed enemies and pursued and destroyed wrongdoers. It was both gracious and malevolent.

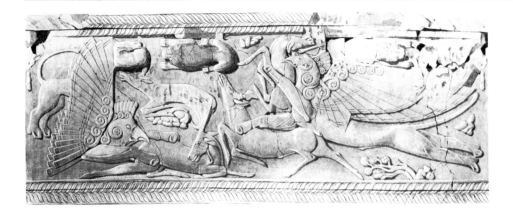

Having passed through many youthful transformations, the Gryphon arrived in Rome, where its shape was formalized and fixed. From that point on – with minor variations – the Gryphon has appeared as we know it today.

Saints, Demons, and Knights

T HE GRYPHON WAS PORTRAYED as both demonic and divine in the art and literature of the Middle Ages. At a time when Christianity used pagan customs and images in its own way and separated an imperfect earth from an ideal heaven, the dual-natured Gryphon became a symbol for both the Devil and for Christ. As a combination of the rapacious eagle and the ferocious lion, the medieval Gryphon represented the Devil and his legions to some. To others, the earthly strength of the lion and the ascendant splendor of the eagle symbolized the earthly and divine natures of Christ.

Opposite: "The Creation of Eve," from Visconti Hours.

Above: In an illustration from the Bodley manuscript, Alexander the Great prepares for his Gryphon flight.

Early in the Middle Ages in Europe, the Gryphon appeared in the company of another figure from the ancient world, Alexander the Great, who conquered Egypt and Persia and invaded India – all countries in which the Gryphon appeared. A champion of Egyptian pharoahs and guardian of Minoan kings, the Gryphon joins Alexander in one of the most popular stories of the Middle Ages. Dating back to before the fourth century, the fanciful *Romance of Alexander* was originally regarded as a history and as a source of information about India and the East.

One of the scenes illustrated in many different manuscripts of the story is Alexander's Gryphon-Flight, or Celestial Journey.

. . . When he came down the mountain,
he ordered his master workers to build
a chair with iron bars on each side. And
four Gryphons were tied to the chair
with iron chains, and over the chair he
put meat, just far enough from the
Gryphons that they flew upward and
carried Alexander into the air. The earth
seemed so small, and the sea looked
like a dragon encircling the earth. Then,
suddenly, God's mysterious veil envel-
oped the Gryphons and forced them to
land in a field, a ten day march from the
army, but Alexander was not hurt.

– THE THORNTON MANUSCRIPT
Translated by Phil Zuckerman

Above: A twelfth-century marble sculpture depicting a guardian Gryphon poised to defend his human charge.

In one version, after reaching the ends of the earth, Alexander longs for new worlds to conquer. One of the remaining worlds is the sky.

After building a chariot-like chair and yoking Gryphons to it, Alexander holds skewers of meat over their heads. As the Gryphons try to move closer to the food, they lift the chariot into the air.

In another version of the story, when the Gryphons pull the conqueror up through the sky, all the birds of the air pay homage to him and he is able to understand their language. In two German versions, the flight is stopped by a heavenly voice which warns him that only those who have performed

good works deserve to ascend to heaven. This is probably to be taken as a Christian condemnation of Alexander's pride. Interpretations of the story – true to the duality of the medieval mind – range from Alexander as Antichrist to his ascent as a symbol of the Resurrection.

A more typically medieval treatment of the Gryphon is to be found in sculpture and in bestiaries, where the Gryphon is usually portrayed as a monster preying upon other animals and men. The so-called "animal meal" was a common motif in ancient art, and the Gryphon's vengeful side was evident in its attack on Pharoah's enemies, in its association with Nemesis, and in its warfare with the Arimaspians.

Above: "La Pieta," a fifteenth-century painting by Bonasia Bartolomeo, in which Gryphons adorn the casket of Christ and assume their traditional role as protectors of the dead.

Above: A felt saddle blanket from the Pazyryk tombs in Siberia. This blanket was buried with other treasures in about 450 B.C. Through the years, water, which leaked into the tomb, froze and preserved much of the contents.

Opposite: Fifteenth-century tapestries depicting Gryphons and other fabulous creatures.

On the right, the Gryphon drives away evil from the famous cathedral, Notre Dame de Paris. On the left, the Gryphon atop the Philadelphia Museum of Art.

Gothic architecture is an expression of the medieval belief that human beings live in a world of sin and danger and that the only salvation is within the Church. The physical cathedral is a symbol of the Church itself, and outside it, in the dangerous world, are gargoyles, Gryphons, and monsters of all kinds, representing the evil powers which attack the soul. Within a single cathedral, though, the Gryphon might be treated in different ways. For example, at St. Mark's, in Venice, the Gryphon attacks a deer in one scene while in another, a pair of Gryphons draws Alexander's chariot through the heavens. The winged lion figure of St. Mark himself is sometimes highly Gryphon-like, as in *The Book of Kells*.

The Griffin is an animal that flies through the air. It is fearsome to see for it has the body and claws of the lion and the wings, head, and fierce beak of the eagle. All men should fear it because it feasts upon them at any opportunity. It is also extremely fond of eating horses. It is seen in these parts but rarely as it lives mostly in high mountains or in Hyperborean lands.

— MEDIEVAL BESTIARY

Above: An eleventh- or twelfth-century French tapestry known as the Bayeux tapestry. This 231-foot tapestry depicts the Norman Conquest of England. Along its borders are Gryphons and other imaginary beasts. At the top, Conan flees. On the bottom, the attack at Dinon is shown.

Preceding page: A detail from Hieronymus Bosch's painting "The Garden of Earthly Delights." The Gryphon is at the top left corner of the painting.

The rapacious nature of the Gryphon is emphasized in medieval bestiaries. The books, derived from what is known as *The Physiologus (The Book of Nature)*, use both actual and fabulous animals to teach Christian lessons, for it was believed that the animals of this world signify the invisible things of God. In bestiary illustrations, the Gryphon often holds a pig, boar, ram, or ox in its claws.

In one medieval story, Gryphons hover over ships, waiting for an opportunity to pluck up with their mighty talons sailors and to carry them off to Gryphon nests and feast upon them. But the sailors, armed with knives, disguise themselves in animal skins. After the Gryphons carry them off to their nests,

the sailors cut their way out of the animal skins and slay the beasts.

Gryphons also try to feast on a young prince in the epic poem, *Gudrun*. During a great celebration in the hall of Sigeband, King of Ireland, the Devil sends his envoy, a Gryphon, to carry away the king's son, Hagen. The Gryphon flies off through the clouds with the screaming child, bearing him to its nest. One of the Gryphon's young picks up the boy and flies off with him to eat him, but Hagen escapes and finds in a cave three royal sisters who have also been abducted by Gryphons. The sisters take him in, feed him, and he remains with them for several years. One day a ship capsizes in a storm

Above: Details from the Bayeux tapestry. At top, Conan surrenders the keys. At bottom, Harold is knighted.

and the sailors and travelers are washed up on shore, where the Gryphons find them and carry them off. Hagen goes down to the beach where he finds a drowned knight. He takes the corpse's armor and weapons and arms himself. At that moment, an old Gryphon swoops down upon him. Hagen shoots arrows at the monster, but does not so much as wound it. As the beast attacks, Hagen slices off one of its wings with a sword. Another Gryphon swoops down upon him, and others after it, and he slays them all. He and the sisters throw the Gryphons into the sea and heap up a mound over the warrior whose weapons had saved him. In time, a ship arrives and rescues Hagen and the princesses.

In the fourteenth century, in Sir John Mandeville's *Travels,* which contains the most famous description of a Gryphon, Mandeville poses as a traveler, describing exotic beings and places. The book is compiled from the works of other writers, and it is doubtful whether the writer — whose real name was probably not Sir John Mandeville — traveled anywhere at all outside his library. In his account, the homeland of Gryphons shifts from the traditional sites of Scythia and India to Bacharie, where trees bear wool like sheep and man-eating *ypotains,* half man and half horse, live sometimes on land and sometimes in water. The tremendous size and strength of the Gryphon is described, focusing on the Gryphon's enormous talons.

Above: A Gryphon's claw. The claw was magic and could be used to cure many diseases.

Opposite: On the fifteenth-century medal by Pisanello at the top, a she-Gryphon nurses human infants. At bottom, a cure for infertility. According to the early German medical manual from which this illustration was taken, by placing a Gryphon on a woman's breast and a fox between her thighs, infertility can be cured.

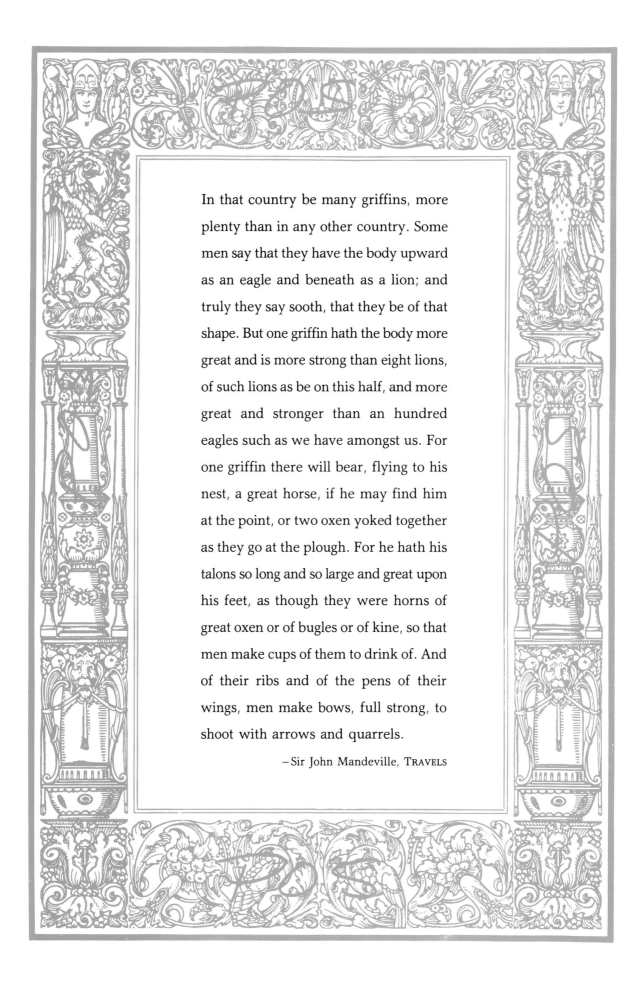

In that country be many griffins, more plenty than in any other country. Some men say that they have the body upward as an eagle and beneath as a lion; and truly they say sooth, that they be of that shape. But one griffin hath the body more great and is more strong than eight lions, of such lions as be on this half, and more great and stronger than an hundred eagles such as we have amongst us. For one griffin there will bear, flying to his nest, a great horse, if he may find him at the point, or two oxen yoked together as they go at the plough. For he hath his talons so long and so large and great upon his feet, as though they were horns of great oxen or of bugles or of kine, so that men make cups of them to drink of. And of their ribs and of the pens of their wings, men make bows, full strong, to shoot with arrows and quarrels.

—Sir John Mandeville, TRAVELS

Above: A twelfth-century mosaic from Palermo.

The claws of the Gryphon can either rip its prey to pieces or aid mankind. During the Middle Ages, a Gryphon's claw, like the horn of a unicorn, was reputed to have magical powers. A claw fashioned into a drinking vessel was believed to change color in the presence of poison. According to legend, the only way a Gryphon claw was acquired was by a holy man who cured a Gryphon of some illness and received the claw as payment for his kindness.

In his description of the Gryphon, Mandeville compares the Gryphon's claws to horns of other animals, and indeed, the Gryphon claws which circulated during the Middle Ages were actually animal horns. In the 1725 edition of Mandeville's

Above: An illustration from Dante's Divine Comedy, *by Federico Zuccari, 1908.*

Travels is a reference to a Gryphon's claw "four foot long" containing the inscription, *Griphi Unguis Divo Cuthberto Dunelmensi sacer* ("Gryphon's talon, sacred to St. Cuthbert of Durham"). This object, now in the British Museum, is actually the horn of an ibex. (Also in the British Museum is a fossilized "Gryphon's egg.") There is said to be a Gryphon's claw from the Holy Land in the Brunswick Cathedral. In the eighteenth century, a surgical instrument used to lift depressed bones of the cranium was called a "griffin's foot."

It was also believed in the Middle Ages that Gryphon feathers, like the feathers of the simurgh, had magical powers. The beneficent Gryphon appears in the tale of a blind king.

The space, surrounded by the four, enclosed

A car triumphal: on two wheels it came,

Drawn at a Gryphon's neck; and he above

Stretch'd either wing uplifted, 'tween the midst

And the three listed hues, on each side, three;

So that the wings did cleave or injure none;

And out of sight they rose. The members, far

As he was bird, were golden; white the rest,

With vermeil intervein'd. So beautiful

A car, in Rome, ne'er graced Augustus' pomp,

Or Africanus'; e'en the sun's itself

Were poor to this . . .

—Dante, THE DIVINE COMEDY
Translated by The Rev. Henry Francis Cary

Above and opposite: Illustration by Sandro Botticelli for the Divine Comedy.

Opposite: At the far right is a detail of a page from a late-fourteenth-century Italian manuscript of the Divine Comedy.

The monarch discovers his eyesight could be restored if a Gryphon feather were passed across his eyes. The king's three sons go and search for the Gryphon King, but only the third son dares to descend to the Gryphon's underground kingdom. The youth serves the Gryphon King in return for a feather and returns to the upper world to restore his father's sight.

The Gryphon's greatest triumph, and vindication, in medieval times was its appearance in Dante's *Divine Comedy*. The Gryphon appears at the summit of the mountain of Purgatory, at what is a turning point in the poem. Dante and his guide, Virgil, have descended through the levels of the Inferno and have climbed the mountain of Purgatory. At the

summit, Dante sees a brilliant light and hears music, the two approaching together. The light becomes a mystical procession, led by the seven spirits of God, followed by elders symbolizing the books of the Old Testament and by four beasts symbolizing the Gospels of the New Testament. Climaxing the procession is the Sacred Gryphon, pulling the triumphal chariot of the Church. There is a peal of thunder, and the procession stops in front of Dante.

The beast that pulled the chariots of Cretan dieties, Apollo, Nemesis, and Alexander the Great pulls the chariot of God and symbolizes the dual nature of Christ. The golden bird parts of the sacred beast represent its divine nature, while its red

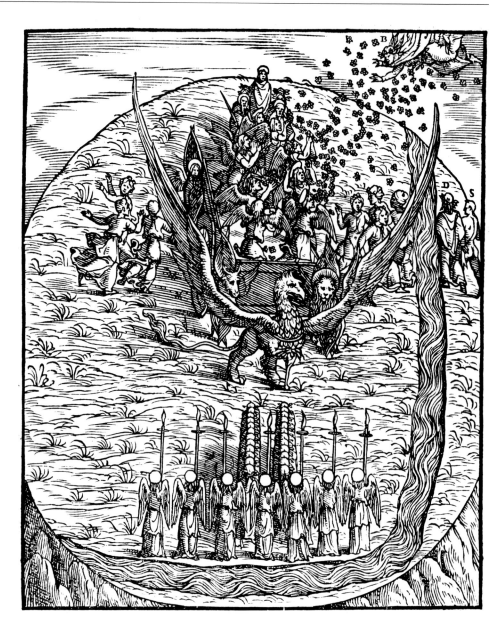

Above: A sixteenth-century Italian woodcut illustration for the Divine Comedy.

and white earthly parts signify human nature. White and red were Dante's colors for the Old and New Testaments, for righteousness and love, and for the body and the soul.

One of the elders calls for Beatrice to appear, the woman Dante loved so much he made her a divine guide in his poem. When she appears, he is overcome, as when he first saw her beside the Arno in Florence, and he turns for support to his guide Virgil. But Virgil, of the ancient world, is gone, unable to ascend higher in the Christian journey. Taking his place as guide is Beatrice, who will accompany Dante the remaining distance, up to the very vision of God. Four dancers, representing the four cardinal virtues, lead Dante to the

Gryphon, where Beatrice is standing, just as the female figures in Minoan art led souls entering the Elysian Fields to an enthroned Gryphon behind which stood the goddess. Looking into the eyes of Beatrice, Dante sees, reflected, the dual-natured Sacred Gryphon, "now in one, now the other guise," the two parts of the nature of Christ.

While Dante is momentarily blinded by the eyes of Beatrice, the procession turns, facing the sun. The procession moves into a wood, Dante following, and stops at a withered tree, the Tree of Knowledge, of which Adam and Eve ate of the Forbidden Fruit. In ancient art, the Gryphon sometimes guarded the Tree of Life and sometimes reached to pluck the

Above: A thirteenth-century Syrian basin, inlaid with silver, showing a Gryphon and other imaginary beasts.

Above: Title page to the German Triumph of Kaiser Maximilliam, *1512.*

Opposite: Fifteenth-century Italian saddle made of stag horn.

fruit of the tree, but now the members of the procession laud the sacred beast:

> . . . *"Blessed thou,*
> *Gryphon! whose beak hath never pluck'd that tree . . .*

and the Gryphon replies: "Yea! for so the generation of the just are saved." Then the beast fastens the pole of the chariot to the withered trunk. Just as plants on earth begin to swell in the light of the sun,

> *"Thus putting forth a hue more faint than rose*
> *And deeper than the violet, was renew'd*
> *The plant, erewhile in all its branches bare."*

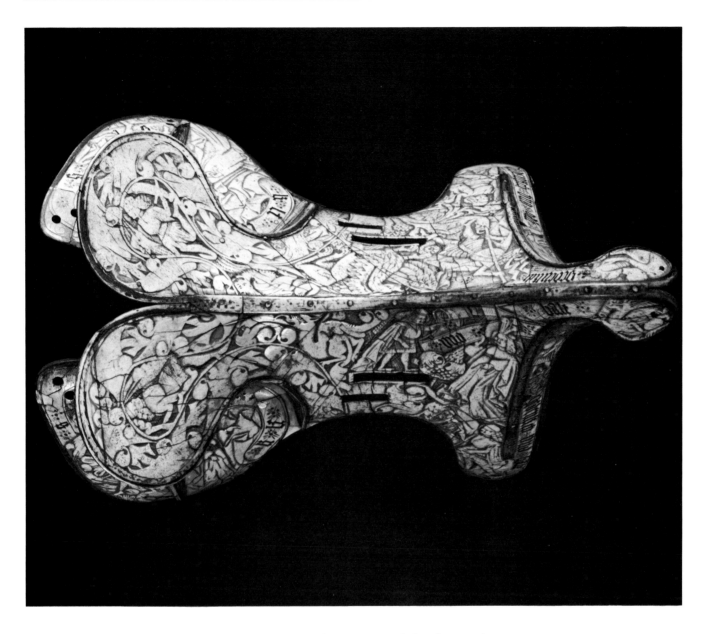

   After The Sacred Gryphon returns the tree to life through
the power of the Church, Dante sleeps, and while he sleeps,
the Gryphon ascends to Paradise.

CHAPTER FOUR

Fabulous and Regal

A S MAN SHIFTED HIS ATTENTION from God and eternal life in heaven to the wonder of man himself and his earthly home, the Gryphon returned to the world.

The monstrous and marvellous, as well as the scientific, fascinated the people of the Renaissance. Christopher Columbus, on one of his voyages to the New World, writes in his log that he saw three sirens leaping about in the sea. The Gryphon became an important figure in heraldry as well as a focal figure in a debate over the existence of fabulous animals.

Opposite: A detail from an engraving by Albrecht Durer, Triumphal Arch of Maximillian I, *1515.*

Heraldry and Coats of Arms

Above: Gryphon supporting the banner of Cardinal Wolsey.

Opposite: At left, the coat of arms of Anne Boleyn. On the right, a scene from the film The Adventures of Robin Hood *with Basil Rathbone.*

When the Gryphon was first portrayed on a coat of arms, it was believed to be an actual beast. In 1167, the beast was emblazoned on the seal of Richard de Revers, Earl of Exeter, but the Gryphon was not widely used again in heraldry until the fifteenth century. A seventeenth-century record of English arms lists sixty-six Gryphons and seventy-three Gryphon heads, and a later heraldic writer lists 290 Gryphons.

The Gryphon appeared on the arms attributed to Alexander the Great, the secret seal of King Edward III, and on the arms of two figures prominently associated with King Henry the

Eighth: one of the king's wives and his cardinal and advisor, Thomas Wolsey. The Gryphon graces the coat of arms of Anne Boleyn and a badge of Cardinal Wolsey, Archbishop of York. It is also on the insignia of the Society of Gray's Inn and is on the Great Seal of the City of London. The Order of the Griffin is a German order of knighthood founded in 1884 by Frederick Francis III of Schewrin. The Gryphon was prominently emblazoned on the arms of the Guy of Gisbourne, played by Basil Rathbone, in the 1938 film *Robin Hood*.

In the late fourteenth century, John de Bado Aureo wrote, "A Griffin borne in arms signifies that the first to bear it was a strong pugnacious man, in whom were found two distinct

Above and opposite: Gryphons used in coats of arms.

natures and qualities, those of the Eagle and the Lion." Possessing the strength of heroes and the splendor of gods, the Gryphon is a natural choice as a heraldic animal. A regal beast, the Gryphon has always been associated with the rulers of earth and sky, from Pharoah and the Cretan kings to Alexander the Great, and even God. Its strength being central to its character, the Gryphon's long lifetime of might and majesty is honored in heraldry.

Characteristics of the Heraldic Griffin

The Gryphon has several special characteristics in heraldry. The sharp ears of the heraldic Gryphon are important. When

only the head of the Gryphon is used, the long pointed ears distinguish it from the head of an eagle. Only the female Gryphon has wings; the wingless male is shown with sharp golden spikes, like rays of light, spreading from its joints.

On coats of arms, the beast is shown in several positions but is most commonly pictured *segreant*, erect with spread wings. The *couchant*, reclining, Gryphon, which appeared so frequently in ancient art, is not common in heraldry.

The Big Debate

The Renaissance love of the fabulous, evident in its love of Gryphons, dragons, wyverns, cockatrices, and unicorns,

Above: On the left, a sixteenth-century Italian dish showing a rampant Gryphon. On the right is a Spanish ceiling tile from the mid-fifteenth century.

reaches its climax in Ariosto's fanciful epic-romance, *Orlando Furioso*. In contrast, Shakespeare's Hotspur, in *Henry the Fourth, Part One*, reacts to such fancies with a rationalistic impatience typical of a growing scientific spirit:

> *. . .Sometimes he angers me*
> *With telling me of the moldwarp and the ant,*
> *Of the dreamer Merlin and his prophesies,*
> *And of a dragon and finless fish,*
> *A clip-winged griffin and a moulten raven,*
> *A couching lion and a ramping cat,*
> *And such a deal of skimble-skamble stuff*
> *As puts me from my faith . . .*

Above: On the left is a detail from a fifteenth-century Italian tribunal. On the right is a detail from a sixteenth-century oak panel from a credence, a small table used to hold the Eucharist.

In 1551, nearly half a century before Hotspur's speech, Konrad Gesner's *Historia Animalium*, a four-volume history of animals, appeared. Its author objectively and conscientiously documented actual animals. The growing interest in scientific inquiry lead to doubts about the Gryphon's existence. Science and traditional belief began to conflict, and the Gryphon was one of the fabulous animals brought to the Court of Science to be put on trial.

THE PROSECUTION In his *Pseudodoxia Epidemica* (*Vulgar Errors*), published in 1646, the English physician Sir Thomas Browne attempts to disprove the existence and prove the

Above: At left, a seventeenth-century Gryphon model carved from wood. At right, a seventeenth-century Italian marriage chest showing the Gryphon as a protector of Ceres, Roman goddess of agriculture.

fabulous nature of many traditional animals, among them, the Gryphon. He lists Aelian, Solinus, Mela, and Herodotus as writers who mention the Gryphon in their works and do not deny its actuality, and Albertus, Pliny, Aldrovandus, and Matthias Michovius as those who declare it a monstrous invention. He points out that the *gryps* mentioned in the Bible is a kind of eagle, and he also contends that the Egyptian Gryphon signifies "the mystical conjunction of hawk and lion." The truth, Browne declares, is that the Gryphon is a symbol, not an actual animal.

THE DEFENSE   Six years later, in *Arcana Microcosmi*, Andrew

Above: A pitcher in the form of a many-winged Gryphon made by Elias Geyer in 1589.

Ross answers Browne, his pages entitled "Dr. Browne's *Vulgar Errors* Refuted and Answered." Ross responds to Browne's chapter on Gryphons with one of his own chapters, "What the Ancients have written of Griffins may be true..."

What follows is a reconstruction of Ross's fanciful argument, his desperate attempt to protect the Gryphon from the attacks of Science:

The Doctor denies that Gryphons exist, but in doing so, he must disprove the writers who he thinks believe in the existence of Gryphons. But he misrepresents those very writers he refers to. Aelian tells us that Gryphons are like Lions in their paws and feet and like Eagles in their wings and head. Solinus says only that

Above: A two-tiered Empire-style table, stamped with the crowned "N" of Napolean Bonaparte, made for his Chateaux de Compeigne.

they are very fierce fowls, Mela that they are cruel and stubborn animals, and Herodotus only mentions their name when he tells of the Arimaspi taking their gold away from them. But none of these writers tell us in plain terms that Gryphons are Lions behind and Eagles in the fore-part.

And even though other writers say that Gryphons are fabulous, their saying so is certainly not sufficient to proving them so, for there are many such 'mixt and dubious' animals in the world. Acosta tells us of the Indian Pacos, which in some parts resembles the Ass, in others the Sheep. Lerius speaks of the Tapiroussou in Brazil, which resembles both an Ass and a Heifer. And there are many other sorts of mixed animals that we read of, such as

Above: A nineteenth-century, mahogany, Empire-style, Pier table with a marble top.

flying Cats, flying Fish, and some sort of Apes with Dogs' heads, called Cynocephali. *Our Bats are partly birds and partly beasts. They fly like a bird with two feet, they walk like a beast with four. They fly with their feet and walk with their wings, some say. And what is even a greater wonder is that there are Plant-animals, or Zoophites, partly plants and partly animals. But the Doctor says, 'In Bats and such mixed animals, there is a commixion of both in the whole rather than an adaptation of the one into the other.' Here he is deceived, for in Bats and such Animals, it is easily seen what parts are of bird and what parts are of beast, which we could not discern if there were a commixion. So, the combination of the two is more of an adaptation. This kind of combination is apparent*

Above: A detail from a seventeenth-century stained-glass window showing the standard for the Guild of Weavers.

in that Indian beast which has the forepart of a Fox, the hind-parts of an Ape, the ears of an Owl, and a bag or purse under its belly where its young ones hide in time of danger.

Nor is it fabulous that these Gryphons are greedy for gold, which they preserve and hide in the earth, for I have seen Magpies do the same thing: I once saw one steal money and hide it in a hole. Maybe this is why Plautus calls Gryphons Mag-pies. But I nonetheless share Aelian's opinion that it is not so much for the gold that the Gryphons fight as for their young ones, which men used to carry away when they searched the country for gold. So it seems that the negative testimony of Michovius is not sufficient to overthrow the received opinion of the Ancients concerning

Above: A stained-glass window from sixteenth-century Switzerland.

Gryphons, especially since there is a possibility in nature for such a compounded animal. For the Gyraffa, or Cameleopard, *is of a stranger composition, being made of the Libbard, Buffe, Hart and Camel.*

Besides, even though some fabulous narratives may have been added to the story of the Gryphons, such as the story of the one-eyed Arimaspi, with whom they fight, it does not therefore follow that there are no Gryphons. If any man say that there are now no such animals to be seen, I answer that that may be so, but simply because they are not seen does not mean they do not exist or that they have perished, for maybe they have moved to places that are more remote and safer because they are inaccessible to

Above: A French casket by Henry Auguste, 1805.

men. And there are many such places, such as in the great and vast countries of Scythia, and Tartaria, and Cathay, where our Europeans never dare, nor could, venture.

THE VERDICT In 1662, ten years after Andrew Ross's refutation of Sir Thomas Browne, England established the Royal Society to foster the new scientific spirit of direct observation and experimentation. The new scientific knowledge gradually discredited the old beliefs.

In a book of the period, *The Museum of Animated Nature*, its author implies that the Gryphon was no longer considered an actual beast. Fantastic descriptions of a gigantic bird, he

writes, "have given place to the moderate details of sober-minded observers, and we no longer look upon this creature as the winged guardian of mountain mines within whose depths were entombed 'gems and barbaric gold,' we no longer imagine it the giant of the winged race, dimming the light of the sun by its widespread pinions, and by the mighty rushing sound as it sweeps down from the sky deafening and stupe-fying the terror-stricken beholders."

Above: On the left, a nineteenth-century porcelain tea urn on a stand. At right, a standing cup with cover, attributed to the German artist David Altonstetter, active 1570-1617.

CHAPTER FIVE

In A Modern Time

T HE DISCREDITED GRYPHON has moved to places more remote. In its modern exile, the beast lives quietly on the edge of imagination.

Alice in Wonderland

In *Alice's Adventures in Wonderland*, the Queen takes Alice to the Gryphon, sleeping in the sun. Commanding the beast to take Alice to hear the Mock Turtle's story, the Queen leaves to oversee executions she had ordered. Alone with the Gryphon, Alice "did not quite like the look of the creature,"

Opposite: Hippogryph by N.C. Wyeth from Legends of Charlemagne.

82

"Of course," the Mock Turtle said, "advance twice, set to partners — "

"Change lobsters, and retire in same order — " interrupted the Gryphon.

"Then, you know," continued the Mock Turtle, "you throw the — "

"The lobsters!" shouted the Gryphon, with a bound into the air.

"As far out to sea as you can — "

"Swim after them!" screamed the Gryphon.

"Turn a somersault in the sea!" cried the Mock Turtle, capering wildly about.

"Change lobsters again!" yelled the Gryphon at the top of its voice, "and then — "

"That's all," said the Mock Turtle, suddenly dropping its voice, and the two creatures, who had been jumping about like mad things all this time, sat down again very sadly and quietly, and looked at Alice.

"It must be a very pretty dance," said Alice timidly.

"Would you like to see a little of it?" said the Mock Turtle.

"Very much indeed," said Alice.

"Come, let's try the first figure!" said the Mock Turtle to the Gryphon, "we can do

Above and opposite: Illustrations by Maurice Sendak for Frank Stockton's The Griffin and the Minor Canon.

Preceding page: From Lewis Carroll's original manuscript for Alice's Adventures in Wonderland, *with original illustrations by Lewis Carroll, dated 1864.*

but decides that she would be as safe with it as with the savage Queen, so she waits. When the Gryphon awakes, its first words are, "What fun!" which, befitting its own dual nature, it speaks "half to itself, half to Alice." Even though this Gryphon is gruff and detached, it becomes the guide of this little Victorian girl, leading her to the Mock Turtle. The Mock Turtle, another composite creature, is pictured as a calf within a turtle's shell. As it sobbingly tells its story, the Gryphon punctuates the tale with puns and an occasional "Hjckrrh!" Then the Mock Turtle mentions the Lobster-Quadrille, and Alice asks what kind of dance that is. The Gryphon and the Mock Turtle gleefully demonstrate the unusual square dance.

Later, when they hear that the trial is beginning, the Gryphon takes Alice by the hand and leads her to the gathering. After the pack of cards flies at her during the mad trial, Alice awakes in her sister's lap and runs home to tea. Her sister, meanwhile, daydreams about Alice's adventures, knowing that soon "the sneeze of the baby, the shriek of the Gryphon, and all the other queer noises, would change . . . to the confused clamour of the busy farm-yard . . ."

The Gryphon and the Minor Canon

Frank Stockton, an American writer, later finds the Gryphon, rich in wisdom and years, living alone "in dreadful wilds

Above: Illustration by Martin Schongauer from fifteenth-century Germany.

scarcely known to man." Hundreds of years before, a sculptor had seen the beast and had carved in stone a likeness of it over the great door of a cathedral in a quiet, faraway town. Learning from some bird or wild animal that there is a likeness of itself on a church in the distant town, the Gryphon decides to travel from its wilderness home and see this likeness, for the Gryphon is the last of its race but does not even know what a Gryphon looks like. After its long journey, its great wings are tired, for it has not made such a long flight in at least a century.

The townspeople are disturbed by the Gryphon's arrival and send their young Minor Canon to speak with the beast and

The Griffin

try to persuade it to leave. Speaking with the Gryphon outside the town, the Minor Canon agrees to show it its likeness
on the church, and thereafter the two become good friends.
The Gryphon, having lived long and seen much, tells the
Minor Canon about "the earth, the air, the water, about
minerals, and metals, and growing things, and all the wonders
of the world!"

Drawn by the friendship of the Minor Canon, the Gryphon
remains in the town, but the people are so afraid of the beast
that they persuade the Minor Canon to leave so that the
Gryphon, following him, will also leave. But the Minor Canon,
without telling the Gryphon he is leaving, goes to the wild

*Above: At the left, an illustra-
tion by H.J. Ford for* The Red
Book of Animal Stories. *On
the right, Arthur Rakham's line
drawing of a Gryphon for Lewis
Carroll's* Alice's Adventures in
Wonderland.

Above: Painting by Douglas Beekman for the book cover of Piers Anthony's The Source of Magic.

alone. Thinking its young friend will return, the Gryphon teaches the cleric's classes, the students improving rapidly because they so fear their new instructor. Fear of the Gryphon also cures the sick, and the poor find jobs. But in spite of the Gryphon's beneficial effect upon the town, the townspeople still fear the beast. To get the Gryphon to leave, an old man tells it that they sent the Minor Canon away, hoping it would follow him. Hearing this, the Gryphon becomes angry, tears its likeness off the church, carries it back to its cave, and sets it beside the entrance. The Gryphon finds the Minor Canon, half-starved in the wild, takes him back to the cave and (as the simurgh befriended Zal) nurses him back to health. Then

the beast carries the Minor Canon back to the town and returns to the wilderness. The Minor Canon becomes respected, even revered, but the Gryphon, lonely for his friend, stops eating, and dies.

Above: Carousel chariot from Lakeside Park, Denver, Colorado.

Yet Gentle Will the Gryphon Be

Belief in the actuality of the Gryphon may be gone as well, but the Gryphon lives on, continuing to change. In Vachel Lindsay's poem, "Yet Gentle Will the Griffin Be (What Grandpa Told the Children)," the Gryphon becomes a chubby, tall-tale animal, lapping up the Milky Way, a world's history away from its role as champion of Pharoah.

Above and opposite: Logotypes using Gryphons.

Just as the Gryphon form has survived through the ages and across the world, so has it survived the transformations of character and personality. The Gryphon is still with us — and not only in the stories and artifacts of the past. With a recent revival of interest in fantasy, the Gryphon has joined other mythical beings as a character in heroic fantasy novels, as a figure in fantasy games, and as a subject for craftsmen.

The Gryphon might well be used as a symbol on spacecraft, so that ages from now, on a distant star, a space traveler may look into the Gryphon's eyes and see the long, rich life of one shape of the human imagination.

GRIFFIN

BOWERS AND RUDDY

BIBLIOGRAPHY

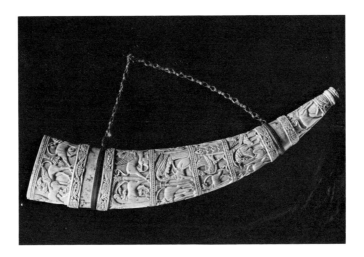

Alighieri, Dante. *The Divine Comedy*. Trans. Laurence Binyon. New York: The Viking Press, 1957.

Armour, Margaret. *Gudrun Done into English*. London: J.M. Dent and Sons, 1932.

Ariosto, Lodovico. *Orlando Furioso*. Trans. Barbara Reynolds. Harmondsworth, England: Penguin Books, 1975.

Bennett, J.A.W., and G.V. Smithers, eds. *Early Middle English Verse and Prose*. Oxford: Oxford University Press, 1968.

Borges, Jorge Luis, with Margaritta Guerro. *The Book of Imaginary Beings*. Trans., Norman Thomas di Giovanni. New York: E.P. Dutton and Company, 1967.

Browne, Sir Thomas. *Pseudodoxia Epidemica*. Vol. II of *The Works of Sir Thomas Browne*. Ed., Charles Sayle. Edinburgh: John Grant, 1912.

Bulfinch, Thomas. *Mythology*. New York: Thomas Crowell, 1913.

Carroll, Lewis. *Alice's Adventures in Wonderland*. New York: Random House, 1946.

Campbell, Joseph. *The Mythic Image*. Princeton: Bollingen Series/Princeton University Press, 1974.

Carter, Dagny. *The Symbol of the Beast; The Animal-Style Art of Eurasia*. New York: Ronald Press, 1957.

Cary, George. *The Medieval Alexander*. Cambridge: Cambridge University Press, 1956.

Chester, Robert. *Love's Martyr*. London, 1611.

Cook, Arthur Bernard. *Zeus*. Vol. II. Cambridge: Cambridge University Press, 1924.

Dawood, N.J., trans. *The Thousand and One Nights*. Baltimore: Penguin Books, 1961.

Davis, William M., trans. "The Romance of Alexander." *Medieval Age*. Ed., Angel Flores. New York: Dell Publishing Company, 1963.

de Gubernatis, Angelo. *Zoological Mythology; or, The Legends of Animals*. London: Trubner and Company, 1872.

Dennys, Rodney. *The Heraldic Imagination*. New York: Clarkson N. Potter, 1975.

Evans, Sir Arthur. *The Palace of Minos*. IV Vols. London: Macmillan and Company, Limited, 1930.

Firdausi. *The Shah Nameh*. Trans. James Atkinson. London: Frederick Warne and Company, 1886.

Franklyn, Julian. *Shield and Crest*. New York: Sterling Publishing, 1961.

Furguson, George. *Signs and Symbols in Christian Art*. New York: Oxford University Press, 1954.

Gardner, Ernest Arthur. *Ancient Athens*. New York: Macmillan Company, 1902.

Gesner, Konrad. *Historia Animalium*. London, 1551-1558.

– – – –. *Curious Woodcuts of Fanciful and Real Beasts*. New York: Dover Books, 1971.

Guerber, H.A. *Legends of the Middle Ages*. New York: American Book Company, 1896.

Herodotus. *The Histories*. Vol. III. Trans., George Rawlinson. New York: D. Appleton and Company, 1860.

Johnson, Samuel. *A Dictionary of the English Language*. London: W. Strahan, 1778.

Lewinsohn, Richard. *Animals, Men and Myths*. New York: Harper and Brothers, 1954.

Lindsay, Vachel. *Collected Poems*. New York: Macmillan and Company, 1925.

Lucretius. *The Nature of the Universe*. Trans., R.E. Latham. Baltimore: Penguin Books, 1957.

Lum, Peter. *Fabulous Beasts*. New York: Pantheon Books, 1951.

McCullock, Florence. *Medieval Latin and French Bestiaries*. Chapel Hill: University of North Carolina Press, 1960.

McHargue, Georgess. *The Beasts of Never*. Indianapolis: Bobbs-Merrill, 1968.

Mandeville, Sir John. *Travels*. (The Cotton MS in modern spelling.) New York: The Macmillan Company, 1905.

Mela, Pomponius. *The Situation of the World*. Trans., Arthur Golding. London, 1585.

Mercatante, Anthony. *Zoo of the Gods*. New York: Harper and Row, 1974.

Mode, Heinz. *Fabulous Beasts and Demons*. Trans., Fabeltiere and Damonen. London: Phaidon, 1975.

Musa, Mark, ed. and trans. *Dante's Purgatory*. Bloomington: Indiana University Press, 1981.

Neumann, Erich. *The Great Mother*. Trans., Ralph Manheim. Princeton: Bollingen Series/Princeton University Press, 1972.

Planche, James Robinson. *The Pursuivant of Arms*. London: Chatto and Windus, 1873.

Pliny (Plinius Secundus, Caius). *Natural History*. Vol. II. Trans., H. Rackham. Cambridge, Mass.: Harvard University Press, 1961.

Polo, Marco. *Travels*. Trans. R.E. Latham. Baltimore: Penguin Books, 1958.

Putnam, Michael C.J. *Virgil's Pastoral Art*. Princeton: Princeton University Press, 1970.

Randall, Richard L., Jr., ed. *A Cloisters Bestiary*. New York: The Metropolitan Museum of Art, 1960.

Richter, Gisela. *A Handbook of Greek Art*. London: Phaidon, 1969.

Robinson, Margaret W. *Fictitious Beasts*. (A bibliography of fantastic animals.) London: Library Association, 1961.

Ross, Alexander. *Arcana Microcosmi*. London, 1652.

Ross, D.J.A. *Illustrated Medieval Alexander-Books in Germany and the Netherlands; A Study in Comparative Iconography*. Cambridge: The Modern Humanities Research Association, 1971.

Rowland, Beryl. *Animals with Human Faces; A Guide to Animal Symbolism*. Knoxville: University of Tennessee Press, 1973.

Schliemann, Dr. Henry. *Mycenae; A Narrative of Researches and Discoveries at Mycenae and Tiryns*. New York: Scribner, Armstrong and Company, 1878.

Shakespeare, William. "Henry the Fourth, Part One." *The Complete Pelican Shakespeare*. Ed., Alfred Harbage. Baltimore: Penguin Books, 1970.

Sisam, Kenneth, ed. *Fourteenth Century Verse and Prose*. Oxford: Oxford University Press, 1967.

Solinus, Julius. *Polyhistoria*. Trans., Arthur Golding. London, 1587.

Stockton, Frank. *The Griffin and the Minor Canon*. New York: Holt, Rinehart and Winston, 1963.

Tawney, C.H., trans. *The Ocean of Story*. (Somadeva's *Katha Sarit Sagara*.) Vol. I. Delhi: Motilal Barrarsidass, 1968.

Thomas, Lewis. *The Lives of a Cell; Notes of a Biology Watcher*. New York: Viking Press, 1974.

Thompson, C.J.S. *The Mystery and Lore of Monsters*. Hyde Park, N.Y.: University Books, 1968.

Vinycomb, John. *Fictitious and Symbolic Creatures in Art*. London: Chapman and Hall Limited, 1906.

Wagner, Dr. W. *Epics and Romances of the Middle Ages*. London: George Routledge and Sons, Limited, 1917.

White, T.H. *The Bestiary; A Book of Beasts*. New York: Putnam's, 1954.

Williams, Charles. *The Figure of Beatrice; A Study in Dante*. New York: Noonday Press, 1961.

Wittkower, Rudolf. *Allegory and the Migration of Symbols*. London: Thames and Hudson, 1977.

Wolohojian, Albert Mugdrich, ed. and trans. *The Romance of Alexander the Great by Pseudo-Callisthenes*. New York: Columbia University Press, 1969.

SOURCES OF ILLUSTRATIONS

FRONT MATTER 3 Courtesy, Museum of Fine Arts, Boston. H.L. Pierce Fund: 9 The J. Paul Getty Museum, Roman mosaic Gryphon: 10 The Metropolitan Museum of Art, Fletcher Fund, 1938 (38.11.3).

CHAPTER ONE 12 Hansmann, Gauting, West Germany: 14 J. Powell, Rome: 15 (left and right) Courtesy, Museum of Fine Arts, Boston. Pierce Fund: 16-17 Scala/Editorial Photocolor Archives: 18 Hansmann, Gauting, West Germany: 19 (left) Courtesy Kelsey Museum of Archaeology, The University of Michigan; (right) Courtesy, Museum of Fine Arts, Boston. William Francis Warden Fund: 20-21 Hansmann, Gauting, West Germany: 22 Hansmann, Gauting, West Germany: 23 The J. Paul Getty Museum, Roman mosaic Gryphon: 24 Hansmann, Gauting, West Germany: 26 J. Powell, Rome: 27 (above) J. Powell, Rome; (below) Courtesy, Museum of Fine Arts, Boston. William E. Nickerson Fund: 28 From Lane, *Arabian Nights*, 1848, NYPL *OFEL: 29 By permission of the Houghton Library, Harvard University: 30 By permission of the Houghton Library, Harvard University: 31 Courtesy, Museum of Fine Arts, Boston. Francis Bartlett Donation of 1900: 32-33 From the Dover Edition of Ariosto's *Orlando Furioso*. Courtesy of Dover Publications, Inc: 34 (left) Mr. and Mrs, Arthur J. Frank, through the courtesy of the Elvehjem Museum of Art, University of Wisconsin-Madison; (right) Courtesy, Museum of Fine Arts, Boston. Gift of Edward Robinson and E.P. Warren by exchange: 35 Asian Art Museum of San Francisco, The Avery Brundage Collection: 36 (left) Courtesy, Museum of Fine Arts, Boston. Gift of Robert B. Osgood; (right) Courtesy, Museum of Fine Arts, Boston. Gift of Mrs. John Gardner Coolidge: 37 Hansmann, Gauting, West Germany.

CHAPTER TWO 38 Courtesy, Museum of Fine Arts, Boston. Gift of Jerome M. Eisenberg: 40 (above left) The Metropolitan Museum of Art, Gift of J. Pierpont Morgan, 1917. (17.190.1686); (above right) Walters Art Gallery, Baltimore; (center) Walters Art Gallery, Baltimore; (below left) Courtesy, Museum of Fine Arts, Boston. Theodora Wilbour Fund in memory of Zoe Wilbour: 41 (from left, clockwise) Courtesy, Museum of Fine Arts, Boston. Anonymous Gift; Courtesy, Museum of Fine Arts, Boston. Catherine Page Perkins Fund; Courtesy, Museum of Fine Arts, Boston. Theodora Wilbour Fund in memory of Zoe Wilbour; Courtesy, Museum of Fine Arts, Boston. Purchased from the Francis Bartlett Donation; Walters Art Gallery, Baltimore; Courtesy, Museum of Fine Arts, Boston. Bartlett Collection; Courtesy, Museum of Fine Arts, Boston: 42 Hirmer Verlag Munchen: 43 Courtesy, Museum of Fine Arts, Boston. Gift of Mrs. S.T. Morse: 44 Museum fur Islamische Kunst. Staatlichemuseen Preussischer Kulturbesitz, Berlin (West), photo – K.H. Paulmann: 45 Asian Art Museum of San Francisco, The Avery Brundage Collection: 46 (top left) Chatillon/Seine, Musee Archeologique. Giraudon; (right) The Toledo Museum of Art, Toledo, Ohio. Gift of Edward Drummond Libbey; (below left) Courtesy, Museum of Fine Arts, Boston. Gift of E.P. Warren: 47 (left and top right) Hirmer Verlag Munchen; (bottom right) Courtesy of The Fogg Museum, Harvard University: 48 Courtesy, Museum of Fine Arts, Boston. Francis Welch Fund: 49 From *200 Decorative Title-Pages*, edited by Alexander Nesbitt, Courtesy of Dover Publications, Inc: 50 Erich Lessing/Magnum Photos: 51 Hirmer Verlag Munchen: 52 Courtesy, Museum of Fine Arts, Boston. Gift of Mrs. Gardner Brewer: 53 American School of Classical Studies at Athens: Agora Excavations.

CHAPTER THREE 54 Biblioteca Nazionale Centrale, Florence. Photo Courtesy of George Braziller, Inc., NY: 56 By permission of the Houghton Library, Harvard University: 57 From *200 Decorative Title-Pages*, edited by Alexander Nesbitt, Courtesy of Dover Publications, Inc: 58 The Cleveland Museum of Art, Gift of the John Huntington Art & Polytechnic Trust: 59 Alinari/Editorial Photocolor Archives: 60 Leningrad Hermitage. Photo Courtesy Tass from Sovfoto: 61 Hansmann, Gauting, West Germany: 62 (left) Philadelphia Museum of Art. Photograph by Robert Neff Longacre, Philadelphia; (right) Alinari/Editorial Photocolor Archives: 63 From *200 Decorative Title-Pages*, edited by Alexander Nesbitt, Courtesy of Dover Publications, Inc: 64-65 Scala/Editorial Photocolor Archives: 66 Bildarchiv Foto Marburg: 67 Bildarchiv Foto Marburg: 68 (above) Elvehjem Museum of Art, University of Wisconsin-Madison, Gift of Vernon Hall; (below) Hansmann, Gauting, West Germany: 69 Hansmann, Gauting, West Germany: 70 From *200 Decorative Title-Pages*, edited by Alexander Nesbitt, Courtesy of Dover Publications, Inc: 71 Alinari/Editorial Photocolor Archives: 72 By permission of the Houghton Library, Harvard University: 73 From *200 Decorative Title-Pages*, edited by Alexander Nesbitt, Courtesy of Dover Publications, Inc: 74 By permission of the Houghton Library, Harvard University: 75 (left) By permission of the Houghton Library, Harvard University; (right) The Pierpont Morgan Library: 76 By permission of the Houghton Library, Harvard University: 77 Courtesy of the Freer Gallery of Art, Smithsonian Institution, Washington, DC: 78 Hansmann, Gauting, West Germany: 79 Courtesy, Museum of Fine Arts, Boston. Centennial Acquisition Fund.

CHAPTER FOUR 80 Courtesy, Museum of Fine Arts, Boston. Otis Norcross Fund: 82 College of Arms MS.I.2, f.9: 83 (left) College of Arms MS.I.2, f.13; (right) Museum of Modern Art/Film Stills Archive, 43rd Street, New York City: 84 By permission of the Houghton Library, Harvard University: 85 By permission of the Houghton Library, Harvard University: 86 Walters Art Gallery, Baltimore: 87 (left) Alinari/Editorial Photocolor Archives; (right) Walters Art Gallery, Baltimore: 88 (left) Hansmann, Gauting, West Germany; (right) The Toledo Museum of Art, Toledo, Ohio: 89 Hansmann, Gauting, West Germany: 90 Courtesy, Museum of Fine Arts, Boston. Gift of Mr. and Mrs. William P. Allis: 91 Courtesy, Museum of Fine Arts, Boston. Purchase price given by W.N. Banks Foundation: 92 Hansmann, Gauting, West Germany: 93 Hansmann, Gauting, West Germany: 94 The Toledo Museum of Art, Toledo, Ohio: 95 (left) Philadelphia Museum of Art, Given by Miss Mary K. Gibson, photographed by the Philadelphia Museum of Art; (right) The Toledo Museum of Art, Toledo, Ohio, Gift of Florence Scott Libbey.

CHAPTER FIVE 96 N.C. Wyeth, *Legends of Charlemagne:* 98 Courtesy of Dover Publications, Inc: 99 Courtesy of Dover Publications, Inc: 100-101 From *The Griffin and the Minor Canon* by Frank R. Stockton. Illustrated by Maurice Sendak. Copyright © 1963 by Maurice Sendak. Reproduced by permission of Holt, Rinehart and Winston, Publishers: 102 The Cleveland Museum of Art, Purchase, Dudley P. Allen Fund: 103 (left) Illustration from *The Red Book of Animal Stories,* edited by Andrew Lang, Reprint Edition published by Charles E. Tuttle Co., Inc: 104 Photo courtesy of Douglas Beekman: 105 Staples & Charles, Washington, DC, photo by Barbara Fahs Charles: 106 (top row) Montalvo Center for the Arts, Saratoga, California; (below left) Heimschutz logo designed by Erwin Reusch (below right) Philadelphia Museum of Art, photographed by Philadelphia Museum of Art: 107 (top row) Reproduced by permission of Canisius College; (below left) Reproduced by permission of Griffin Publishing Company, Inc; (below middle) Griffin Design Registered Trademark of Western Publishing Company, Inc. Used by permission; (below right) Copyright Bowers & Ruddy Galleries, Los Angeles, CA: 109 Courtesy, Museum of Fine Arts, Boston. Marie Evans Fund.